Rhodes Rage

Cartoons from *Mail & Guardian*, *Sunday Times* and *The Times*

JACANA

Acknowledgements: Thanks to Mike Wills for once again writing canny captions and whipping the book into shape; thanks to my editors at the Mail & Guardian *(Angela Quintal, Moshoeshoe Monare), at the* Sunday Times *(Phylicia Oppelt) and at* The Times *(Stephen Haw) and their production staff; thanks to Guy Jepson for the smart headline that became this book's title; my website, ePublications and rights manager, the tireless Richard Hainebach; my invaluable assistant Eleanora Bresler; Roberto for colour editing; Bridget Impey, Russell Martin and all at Jacana including Kerrie Barlow for managing production one last time; Claudine Willatt-Bate for layout; and as always on the home front, Nomalizo Ndlazi and my family: Karina, Tevya and Nina.*

10 Orange Street
Sunnyside
Auckland Park 2092
South Africa
(+27 11) 628 3200
www.jacana.co.za

in association with

© Jonathan Shapiro, 2015

ISBN 978-1-4314-2255-5

Cover design by Jonathan Shapiro

Page layout by Claudine Willatt-Bate
Printed and bound by ABC Press, Cape Town
Job no. 002607

See a complete list of Jacana titles at www.jacana.co.za

See Zapiro's list and archive at www.zapiro.com

For our bastion of courage,
the Arch

ZAPIRO annuals

The Madiba Years (1996)

The Hole Truth (1997)

End of Part One (1998)

Call Mr Delivery (1999)

The Devil Made Me Do It! (2000)

The ANC Went in 4x4 (2001)

Bushwhacked (2002)

Dr Do-Little and the African Potato (2003)

Long Walk to Free Time (2004)

Is There a Spin Doctor In the House? (2005)

Da Zuma Code (2006)

Take Two Veg and Call Me In the Morning (2007)

Pirates of Polokwane (2008)

Don't Mess With the President's Head (2009)

Do You Know Who I Am?! (2010)

The Last Sushi (2011)

But Will It Stand Up In Court? (2012)

My Big Fat Gupta Wedding (2013)

It's Code Red! (2014)

Other books

The Mandela Files (2008)

VuvuzelaNation (2013)

DemoCrazy (2014)

26 September 2014

Zuma's been in Moscow for private chats with Putin; the Russians and our energy ministry surprisingly announce a deal to build nuclear reactors; then Mac Maharaj's spin starts

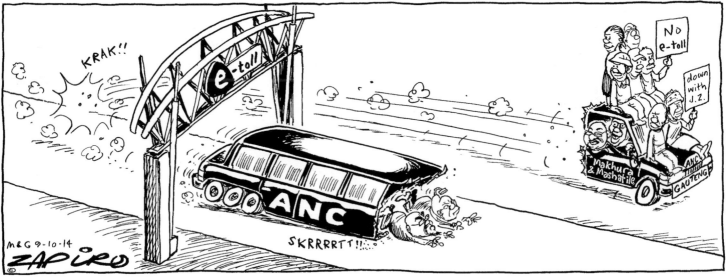

9 October 2014

Gauteng ANC heavyweights David Makhura and Paul Mashatile
break party ranks on unpopular e-tolling and call for review

12 October 2014

At the ineffectual Seriti Commission, indefatigable arms deal critic Terry Crawford-Browne airs rumours about the deaths of Chris Hani and Joe Modise sourced from discredited ANC spy Bheki Jacobs

7

THE TIMES 14·10·14
ZAPIRO

14 October 2014

Two years after the Taliban shot her for attending school,
Pakistani activist Malala Yousafzai becomes youngest-ever Nobel laureate at 17

8

Pistorius lacked 'dolus eventualis' so he's only guilty of culpable homicide; hip hop star
'Jub Jub' Maarohanye's murder conviction for killing children in drag racing accident is overturned;
now prosecution case against Shrien Dewani for allegedly masterminding his wife's killing is on the rocks.

16 October 2014

19 October 2014   Speculation on Pistorius sentencing veers between 15 years in prison and a correctional wrist slap

STARDOM

WEALTH

$

FAME

GO TO JAIL.

SHORT SENTENCE

THE TIMES 23-10-14
ZAPIRO ©

23 October 2014   Five years in prison it is … but his lawyer expects that to mean ten months inside and the rest on parole

20 October 2014

30 October 2014   National outrage as Bafana Bafana and Orlando Pirates goalkeeper and captain is murdered in Vosloorus

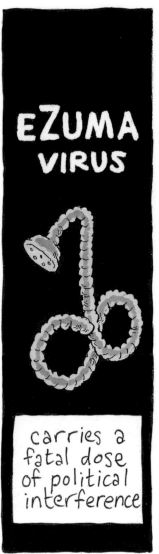

Ebola is rampant in West Africa. Government's desire to control media is spreading here. Sacked e.tv boss Marcel Golding says holding company director and Zuma crony Yunus Shaik tried to influence news content.

30 October 2014

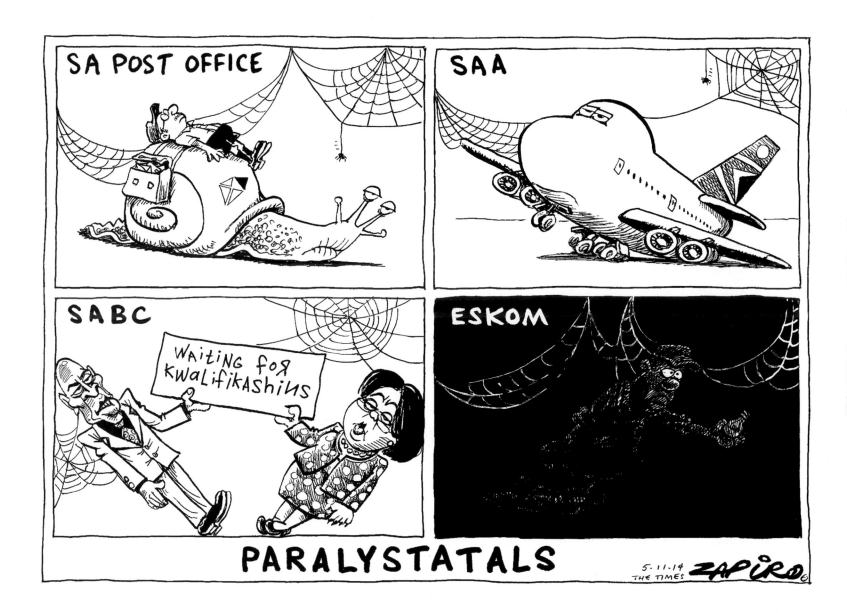

5 November 2014

Axed and disgraced former national police commissioner stokes campaign
for him to return and replace blundering incumbent Riah Phiyega

9 November 2014

Steve Hofmeyr somehow gets a court order gagging comedian Conrad Koch
from talking about him, but Koch keeps tweeting from his famous puppet's handle

17

IN THE NEWS:...

...A TWITTER HARASSMENT LAWSUIT— AGAINST A PUPPET!

...BROUGHT BY A SINGER...

...WHO'S PROUDLY RACIST TILL THE PUPPET COSTS HIM.

BIZARRELY, A MAGISTRATE BUYS THE ARGUMENT!

THE SINGER, TOO CHICKEN TO FACE THE PUPPET IN COURT...

...SENDS AN 'ACADEMIC' WHO DOES STAND-UP COMEDY WITHOUT TRYING...

...ALLEGING THE PUPPET'S IN A 'MARXIST LEFTIST CONSPIRACY'!

LAUGHED OUT OF COURT, THE 'ACADEMIC' ASSAULTS THE PUPPET!

Today's cartoon authored by REALITY.

Legal twar ends up in court

PARLIAMENTARY TERMS (REVISED)

16 November 2014

On orders of speaker Baleka Mbete, riot police enter
National Assembly and forcibly remove EFF members

21 November 2014   Controversial public artwork appears on Sea Point promenade looking out at Robben Island

23 November 2014

Deputy President Cyril Ramaphosa tasked with
getting parties working together to restore a functional parliament

26 November 2014

Opposition wants answers on Public Protector's report about massive overspending
on his Nkandla homestead but he's refusing to face the parliamentary music

Women drugged and raped by the squeaky clean Bill Cosby over nearly half a century start speaking out − nearly twenty of them and counting

20 November 2014

27 November 2014

Mbeki tried to keep it under wraps but *Mail & Guardian* reveals damning
Khampepe report into 2002 Zimbabwean elections which says they weren't free and fair

2 December 2014

25

4 December 2014

SABC chair nailed by a parliamentary committee for misrepresenting her academic record and lying when she said her degree documentation was stolen

5 December 2014
First anniversary of Mandela's death

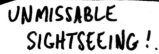

Beautiful CAPE TOWN!

UNMISSABLE SIGHTSEEING!..

UNMATCHED MOUNTAINS!..

UNRIVALLED BEACHES!...

...AND UNTRANSFORMED SUBURBAN RACISM

ASSAULTED BY CYCLIST SHOUTING "GET OFF MY STREET!"

Cynthia Joni, domestic worker, Kenilworth

SJAMBOKKED BY BMW DRIVER WHO "MISTOOK HIM FOR A THIEF"

Muhammed Makungwa, gardener, Claremont

URINATED ON FROM A NIGHTCLUB BALCONY BY A STUDENT "YOU'RE BLACK, I'M WHITE, YOU'RE POOR, I'M RICH!"

Michelle Puis Nomgcana, taxi driver, Claremont

tripadvisor: CAREFUL OF SWIMMING WHILE DRUNK OR WALKING WHILE BLACK

7-12-14
SUN.TIMES

ZAPIRO

7 December 2014

9 December 2014

Judge acquits, saying prosecution's evidence fell far below required threshold
for the trial to proceed. Anni's sister says 'the justice system has failed us'.

FAMILY STEAL

The doctor who did Steve Biko's autopsy nearly 40 years ago had given the final report to his private secretary for safekeeping ... now her children try to auction it off

10 December 2014

11 December 2014   90-year-old president undermines heir apparent and promotes his wife into Women's League presidency

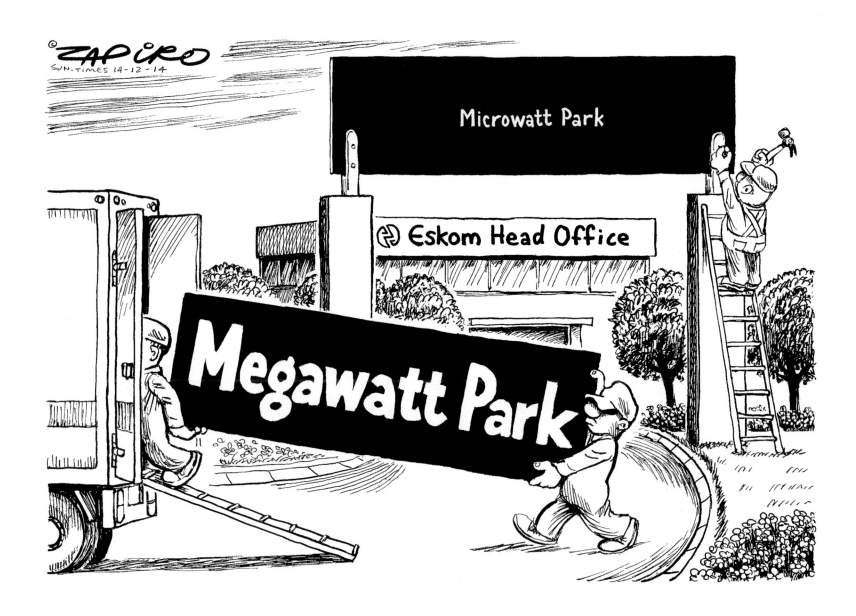

14 December 2014   Embattled electricity supplier admits that power cuts will continue for months

21 December 2014

17 December 2014

11 January 2015

Mass solidarity in Paris and around the world for the twelve people – cartoonists and staff –
massacred by Muslim extremists at French satirical newspaper's office

D.I.Y. Freedom of Expression

Je suis CHARLIE

thanks PDU
M&G 15-1-15
ZAPIRO

15 January 2015

36

© ZAPIRO
THE TIMES 15-1-15

Proclaiming solidarity,
Nigeria's Goodluck Jonathan

Je suis CHARLIE

BOKO HARAM VICTIMS

15 January 2015

Quick to damn Paris atrocity, Nigerian president stays silent on recent attacks
by Islamic extremists Boko Haram costing hundreds of lives in his own country

18 January 2015

Journalists or party hacks? A pair of senior Survé editorial bosses
seen in ANC regalia at the 103rd birthday celebrations.

20 January 2015

Author of best-selling memoir on her life as Madiba's PA lets fly with
some racial vitriol on Twitter under the profile name Zelda van Riebeeck

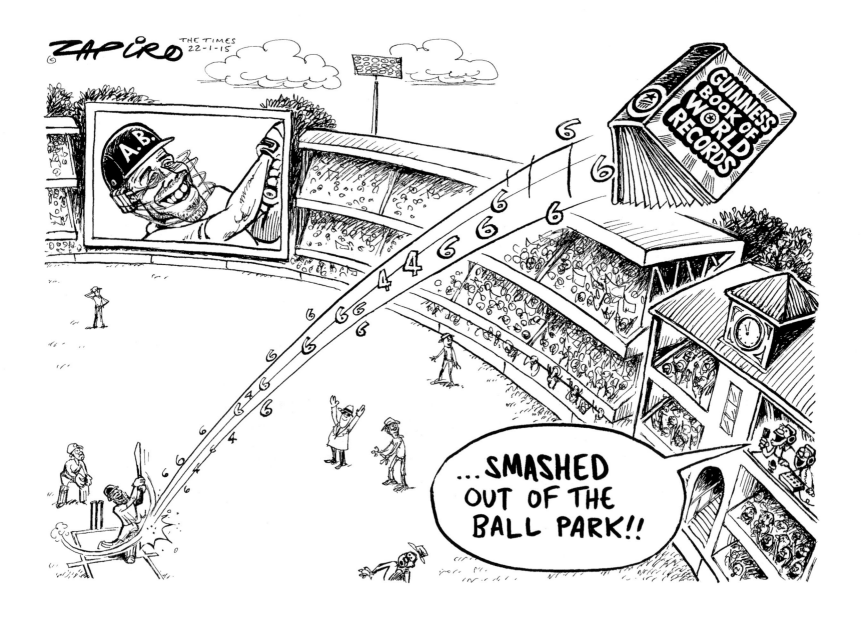

22 January 2015   Proteas' skipper blasts the Windies for the fastest ODI century ever in just 31 balls

25 January 2015

Foreign-owned shops in Soweto are looted and destroyed
but Gauteng MEC for Safety says it's not what it seems

41

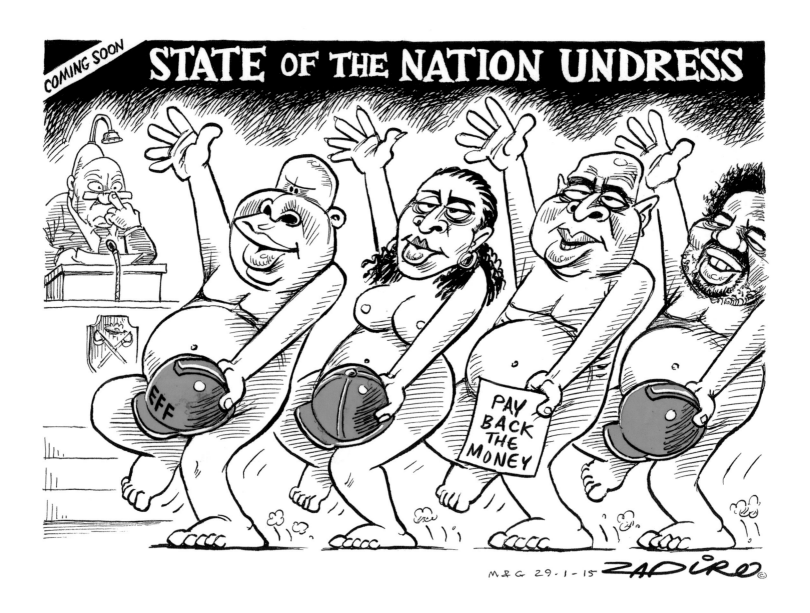

29 January 2015

Two weeks before president's big annual address, EFF MPs threaten to go naked into
the chamber in defiance of parliamentary ban on their trademark red overalls and miners' hats

29 January 2015   Special Investigating Unit head Vas Soni resigns after completion of report into Nkandla spending

FREE...

1 February 2015

Sentenced to two life sentences plus 212 years in prison on 89 charges including six counts of murder, apartheid's Prime Evil is out on parole after serving 20 years

ROAD RENAMING CEREMONY...

DE KOCK

NOBEL

ZAPIRO M&G 5-3-15

5 March 2015

De Kock has reason to believe he was the fall guy for Nat leaders like
FW de Klerk who is honoured with a Cape Town highway in his name

45

3 February 2015

At disgraced former national police commissioner's funeral, Mbeki and ANC
deputy secretary-general Jessie Duarte laud his achievements and tout conspiracy theories

8 February 2015

Mugabe trips over a poorly-laid red carpet and the hapless image goes viral

12 February 2015   Eve of SONA

SONA chaos. Mystery device jams cell phone signals. Deliberately not covered by SABC TV feed, plainclothes cops dressed like waiters violently eject EFF members. Other opposition parties walk out. Zuma giggles, then delivers stilted speech.

15 February 2015

22 February 2015

Who jammed the signal in parliament? Not I, said the Speaker. Not us, said the ministers.
State Security Minister David Mahlobo says the culprit will be found.

19 February 2015

A LESSON IN METAPHOR FOR BALEKA MBETE

This is a **CARTOON**. It's also a **METAPHOR**. No newspaper reader will think you are **actually a disgusting insect** — it's just your **bullying abuse of power** that's disgusting.

But there's nothing funny about calling someone a **COCKROACH** at a **political rally**, where followers tend to take things **literally**.

ANC

You know that **ONE MILLION PEOPLE** were **slaughtered** in the **1994 RWANDA GENOCIDE** after ruthless politicians ethnically labelled them **COCKROACHES**

Here's your **EXTENDED METAPHOR** (if applied to **you**).

Not so funny **now**, hey?

THE TIMES 17-2-15

ZAPIRO

17 February 2015

Addressing an ANC rally, the Speaker says 'if we don't work we will continue to have cockroaches like Malema roaming all over the place'

52

24 February 2015

New party fractures with suspension of Andile Mngxitama and two other
MPs for airing allegations of financial mismanagement against Malema

20 February 2015

26 February 2015

Largest SA intelligence leak in decades sees *Al Jazeera*
and *The Guardian* running hugely embarrassing stories

27 February 2015

1 March 2015

The *Sunday Times* reports that one of the president's wives, MaNtuli,
was 'exiled' from Nkandla after allegedly being linked to a poison plot against him

CAPE TOWN FIRES

NO-CONFIDENCE VOTE

PARLIAMENT

THE TIMES 4·3·15
ZAPIRO

4 March 2015   Zuma feels the heat in the National Assembly as firefighters battle blazes across the Peninsula

6 March 2015

Israel's Prime Minister Binyamin Netanyahu goes behind Obama's back
to stir support in Congress for his hardline position on Tehran

MISSION:IMPROBABLE

Mahlobo

State
Security
Agency

GOOD MORNING. YOUR MISSION, SHOULD YOU CHOOSE TO ACCEPT IT, IS TO **PRETEND** THAT **MADONSELA, MALEMA** AND **LINDIWE MAZIBUKO** ARE GENUINELY **SUSPECTED** OF BEING **C.I.A. AGENTS.**

THIS MESSAGE — ALONG WITH YOUR LAST SHRED OF CREDIBILITY — WILL SELF-DESTRUCT IN FIVE SECONDS...

SUN.TIMES 8.3.15 ZAPIRO ©

8 March 2015

Seriously, the minister says there's an official inquiry underway
into loopy anonymous cyber allegations against government irritants

10 March 2015

Another legal setback, but the president's wealthy nephew still refuses
to take any responsibility for the collapse of his mining venture

13 March 2015

Officials say the Western Cape town's new card system is simply
to identify outsiders with legitimate jobs. Sounds familiar.

13 March 2015   Exposed for the third time, the designer's protestations are wearing thin

15 March 2015

His exercise partner is awaiting-trial mobster Radovan Krejcir

65

17 March 2015   High-speed blue-light crash claims well-respected minister in the presidency and mbira musician

20 March 2015   UCT student Chumani Maxwele throws faeces on the campus statue, igniting vitriolic debate

26 March 2015

Loudmouth Top Gear presenter in trouble yet again.
Decking a producer on set gets him finally axed by the BBC.

29 March 2015

22 March 2015

Western Cape cabinet instructs all departments not to renew
Cape Times subscriptions because of 'shoddy journalism'

25 March 2015   Tennis legend found guilty of rape and sexual assault on young girls he coached decades ago

27 March 2015   Another weird statement from the president — 'If I was a dictator I would change a few things …'

31 March 2015

Local comedian gets top American gig

2 April 2015

Boy band hits town

2 April 2015

Union federation central executive committee, controlled by Zuma allies, finally votes to dismiss outspoken general secretary Zwelinzima Vavi. The movement seems set to split.

5 April 2015

Deputy head of the prosecuting authority weighs in on Number One's case
saying key Mbeki supporters used the NPA to fight political battles

Another flurry. EFF members deface Paul Kruger's statue in Pretoria with green paint.
Afrikaans singer threatens to chain herself to the statue if the vandalism doesn't stop.

9 April 2015

10 April 2015   Rhodes statue at UCT is removed as colonial memorials across the country are targeted

14 April 2015   A month before party leadership elections, surprise announcement that she'll step down

12 April 2015

Attacks on foreigners in KZN after Zulu King Goodwill Zwelithini says
they dirty the streets and should go back to their own countries

16 April 2015

17 April 2015   The King slams the media for mistranslation, belatedly calls for peace and holds anti-xenophobic imbizo

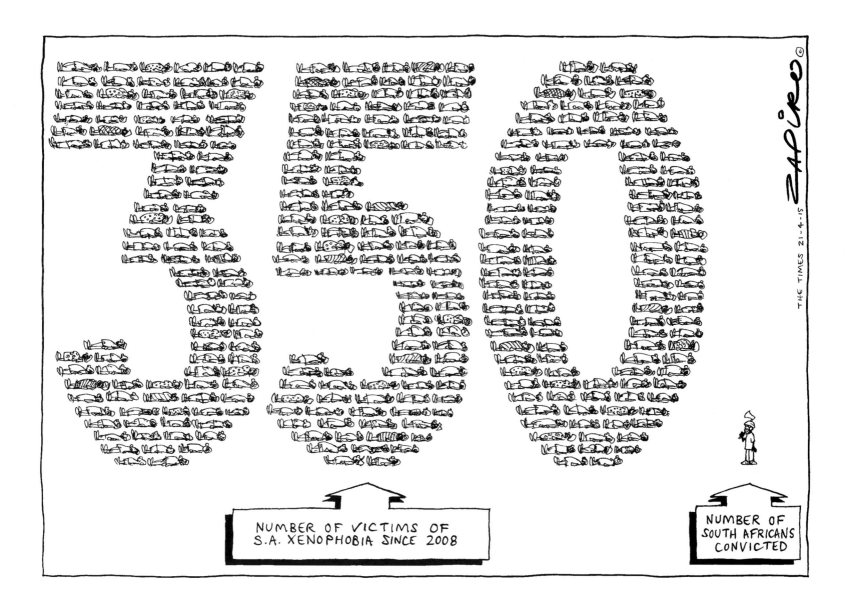

NUMBER OF VICTIMS OF S.A. XENOPHOBIA SINCE 2008

NUMBER OF SOUTH AFRICANS CONVICTED

21 April 2015

Much-loved Kaizer Chiefs star and hero of Bafana Bafana's
1996 AFCON Cup winning team succumbs to stomach cancer

23 April 2015

26 April 2015   Transnet boss Brian Molefe is the new temporary chief executive … the third inside a year

ZAPIRO 28-4-15 THE TIMES

28 April 2015   Freedom Day

30 April 2015

Wits student council president is unapologetic about
Facebook posts expressing love and admiration for Nazi leader

8 May 2015

30 April 2015   DA leadership election TV debate – the glitzy 'Soweto's Obama' vs erudite but dour Dr James

The Temptation of Pastor Maimane

ZAPIRO
THE TIMES 7-5-15

CONSTITUTIONALISM

The Constitution

LEADER?!

Death penalty referendum

POPULISM

7 May 2015

In the TV debate, Maimane expresses some views more in line with
his background as a lay preacher than with his party's liberal principles

Right2Know report says intelligence agencies are monitoring and infiltrating civil society groups

When **ASSISTED SUICIDE** comes before the Concourt, what **evidence** should the court consider?

☐ **a.** The patient's right to die with dignity

☐ **b.** Doctors' evidence on quality of life

☐ **c.** Constitutional right to dignity

...or ☐ **d.** Ancient instruction manual dictated by imaginary friend in the sky

5·5·15
THE TIMES   ZAPIRO ©

5 May 2015   Religious groups oppose Cape Town advocate seeking court order allowing him to die with the help of his doctors

10 May 2015 — Six years after his death's door release on medical parole, the golf-loving fraudster wants greater freedom

12 May 2015

In a tribute speech to Helen Zille that backfires, the veteran journalist lists
apartheid's architect among the 'really smart politicians' he has known

15 May 2015

Newly elected DA leader's profile-raising campaign is trending

President wants prosecutions head Mxolisi Nxasana out but he fights for his job, accusing top lieutenants like Nomgcobo Jiba of using state resources to dig up dirt on him

14 May 2015

17 May 2015   Burundi's president thwarts coup attempt sparked by his intention to defy a two-term limit

20 May 2015

Australian authorities issue a 'deport or destroy' order on the star's pets
which he imported illegally while filming the latest episode of his famous series

Good news! e-tolls reduced!

GOVT

21 May 2015   Misplaced optimism. Cyril believes new deal he brokered on e-tolls will be well received.

Cops accused of brutally targeting foreigners in their co-ordinated 'sweep clean' activities
while the home affairs minister goes gimmicky with a new set of awards

22 May 2015

100

24 May 2015

Judge Farlam handed over his findings nearly two months ago

28 May 2015

Acting on instructions from the Americans, Swiss authorities arrest high-ranking
FIFA officials for allegedly receiving bribes. Supremo Sepp Blatter is 'not under investigation'.

29 May 2015

IF IT WALKS LIKE A...

AND QUACKS LIKE A...

...IT'S PROBABLY A...

SA implicated in US charges against FIFA, but 2010 world cup boss Danny Jordaan claims altruistic purpose for $10m paid to notoriously corrupt Caribbean Football Union during our successful bid process

2 June 2015

5 June 2015

As ever, the sports minister huffs and puffs

7 June 2015

Thabo Mbeki is dragged into the scandal alongside the bid committee –
documents show the then president agreed to the $10m payment in discussions with Blatter

Surprise resignation

31 May 2015

Comical video produced by ministers to show that everything at the president's residence is essential for security. They say Zuma owes nothing and even more must be spent to maintain standards.

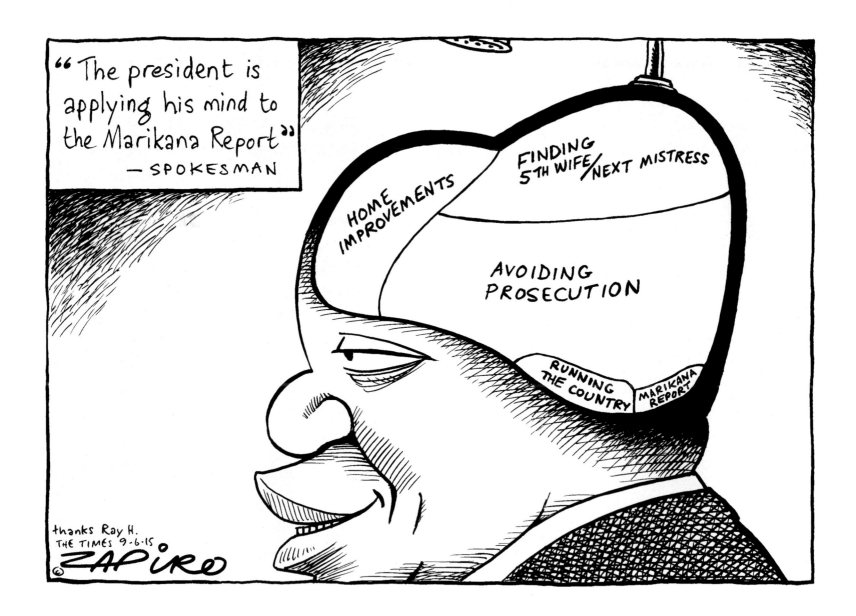

9 June 2015

10 June 2015

Just eight months into his sentence, Oscar is approved for parole

Senior advocate in Zuma case makes startling revelation

14 June 2015

ANC Gauteng chair Paul Mashatile becomes the first senior
party official to publicly distance himself from Nkandla spending

Hollow Man (contd.)

SA PRINCIPLES

AIR GENOCIDE

al-Bashir

THE TIMES 18·6·15

ZAPIRO

Government brazenly flouts Pretoria court order and colludes in departure from SA
of Sudanese president, wanted by International Criminal Court for Darfur war crimes

18 June 2015

114

21 June 2015

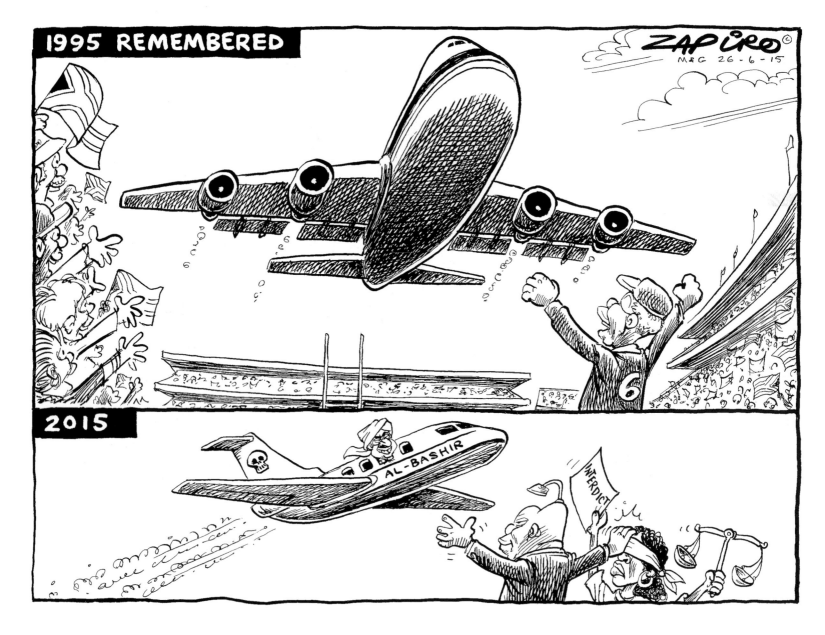

26 June 2015

20th anniversary of Rugby World Cup triumph

EFF's PARLIAMENTARY RECORD

Disruptive tactics are wearing thin

The latest in a spate of racially based killings in the US – Dylan Roof, fuelled by
Ku Klux Klan hatred, murders nine African American churchgoers in South Carolina

25 June 2015

28 June 2015

OMISSION OF INQUIRY

1 July 2015   The cops cop all the blame. The politicians are off scot free.

3 July 2015

Greek financial crisis with EU gets serious

3 July 2015

Greek PM calls a snap poll on whether the country should accept
tough bailout conditions imposed by German leader Angela Merkel

19 July 2015

Seems the passenger rail body bought locomotives worth R3.5bn that
don't meet our safety specs and the chief engineer faked his qualifications

23 July 2015   Defending the indefensible. Police minister's findings on Nkandla are savaged by opposition MPs.

26 July 2015

Parliamentary committee does *in situ* inspection

31 July 2015   Comedian Conrad Koch's alter ego gets lost for a while on the way home from Canada

28 July 2015   Soshanguve pastor exposed for feeding snakes to his followers in the name of their salvation

Malusi Gigaba claims he's tackling child trafficking but devastates tourism
with strict requirements on parents for unabridged birth certificates

30 July 2015

Obama's on an African tour chiding the continent's political leaders for power-hungry behaviour
but it's the illegal shooting of Zimbabwe's Cecil the lion by an American dentist which grabs headlines

2 August 2015

7 August 2015   Malema's corruption case is struck off the Polokwane High Court roll because of numerous postponements

130

4 August 2015

Leaked blood tests plunge world athletics into crisis

6 August 2015   Provincial police commissioners publicly support their boss who's facing an inquiry in the wake of Farlam Report

9 August 2015   Annual talk-a-thon launched

13 August 2015   'Look like a girl. Act like a lady. Think like a man. Work like a boss.' What was Bic thinking?

14 August 2015   After a humiliating first-ever loss to Argentina, Bok coach is under pressure on and off the field

16 August 2015

Third anniversary of the massacre

20 August 2015   Party admits failings in a mid-term review document, but you-know-who isn't mentioned

18 August 2015

Boycott Disinvestment & Sanctions activist Muhammed Desai is told he cannot wear his campaign T-shirt at the gym. After a Free Speech uproar they change their mind.

21 August 2015

New NPA boss Shaun Abrahams withdraws charges against his deputy
Nomgcobo Jiba and strengthens her position within the organisation

140

23 August 2015

25 August 2015   Concern as the 83-year-old icon is hospitalised

27 August 2015

This time Thuli nails the former PRASA boss for improper conduct

28 August 2015   400m winner at the world champs

144

Deputy president flies expensively to Japan on a chartered jet
owned by the Guptas and the president's son Duduzane

30 August 2015

1 September 2015

To the surprise of critics, Chief Justice Mogoeng Mogoeng
confronts the president on political intimidation of the courts

3 September 2015

Swazi king callously proceeds with his archaic ritual selection

4 September 2015   SABC boss Motsoeneng again calls for media regulation and makes an eyepopping claim

8 September 2015

Searing image of the three-year-old Syrian boy Aylan Kurdi
washed up on a Turkish beach re-defines the European refugee crisis

SUN. TIMES 6.9.15 ZAPiro

6 September 2015

10 September 2015

Deputy minister says abolition of dual citizenship is on the agenda
because it's been abused by SA citizens fighting for Israel

11 September 2015

Scientists reveal extensive remains of a new human
ancestor species *Homo naledi* discovered in Gauteng

13 September 2015

ANC chief whip says *Homo naledi* and palaeontology represent
pseudo-science based on Western materialist world-view

Pretoria High Court rejects government appeal against flouted order
barring Sudan's dictator from leaving the country in June

17 September 2015

154

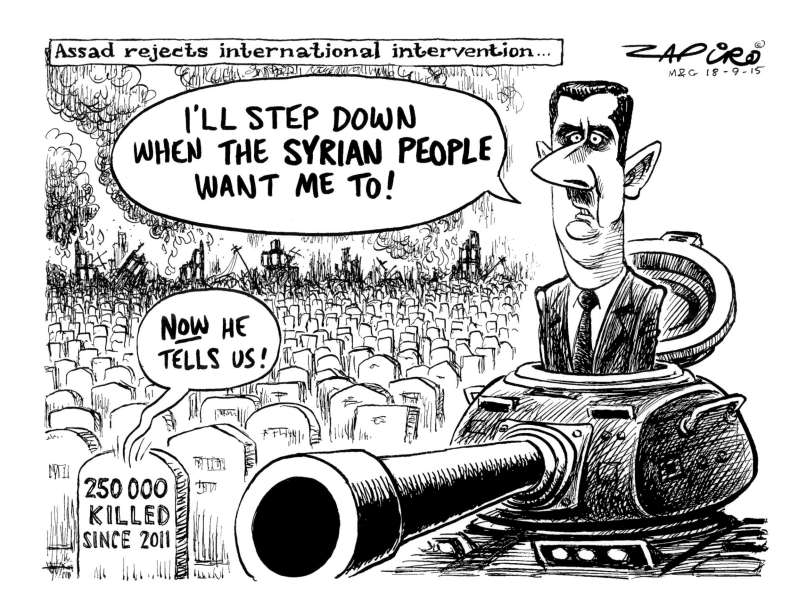

18 September 2015

　Defending champions overwhelming favourites at the start of Rugby World Cup in England

22 September 2015   Bok's shock 34–32 loss to Japan's underestimated 'Brave Blossoms' is the biggest upset in rugby history

24 September 2015 Surprise ministerial appointment Mosebenzi Zwane has links to notorious influence peddlers

27 September 2015   German car giant exposed for deliberate systematic cheating of US emissions tests

29 September 2015   Zuma on world stage at UN General Assembly. Who knew?